Rigoberta Menchú Túm

Champion of Human Rights

By Julie Schulze

John Gordon Burke Publisher, Inc.

Contemporary Profiles and Policy Series for the Younger Reader
Next in the series: Nancy Landon Kassebaum

This book is dedicated to Debby and the future peacemakers of Central America

Library of Congress Cataloging-in-Publication Data

Schulze, Julie, 1943–

   Rigoberta Menchú Túm : champion of human rights / by Julie Schulze.

      p. cm. — (Contemporary profiles and policy series for the younger reader)

      Includes bibliographical references and index.

      Summary: A biographical account of the Quiché Indian woman from Guatemala who won the Nobel Peace Prize in 1992 in recognition of her work for social justice.

      ISBN 0–934272–42–5 (cloth : alk. paper). — ISBN 0–934272–43–3 (pbk. : alk. paper)

      1. Menchú, Rigoberta—Juvenile literature. 2. Quiché women—Biography—Juvenile literature. 3. Human Rights Workers—Guatemala—Biography—Juvenile literature. 4. Mayas—Guatemala—Government relations—Juvenile literature [1. Menchú, Rigoberta. 2. Quiché Indians—Biography. 3. Indians of Central America—Guatemala—Biography. 4. Women human rights workers. 5. Human rights workers. 6. Guatemala. 7. Women—Biography.] I. Title. II. Series.
F1465.2.Q5M388 1997

972.81'004974

[B]–DC21   97–35470

                                                                                                      CIP

                                                                                                      AC

Credits: Chapter quotations from Rigoberta Menchú Túm and I, Rigoberta Menchú, An Indian Woman in Guatemala; Line drawings of Rigoberta Menchú Túm: Amy Harlan-Blount; Map of Guatemala: Cartesia Software.

Copyright © 1997 by John Gordon Burke Publisher, Inc.

TABLE OF CONTENTS

INTRODUCTION: CHAMPION OF HUMAN RIGHTS

"What I treasure most in life is being able to dream. During the most difficult moments and complex situations, I have been able to dream of a more beautiful future."

Many people were puzzled when the Oslo, Norway-based, Nobel Prize panel announced to the world that Rigoberta Menchú Tum would receive the 1992 Nobel Peace Prize. After all, Nobel prizes had been awarded since 1901, and most of the previous winners had been men who were well established in their work.

In 1992, however, this unknown young Mayan Indian woman from Guatemala, barely 33 years old, claimed the $1.2 million prize and joined the ranks of history, along-side Martin Luther King, Jr. of the United States, Bishop Desmond TuTu of South Africa, and Mikhail Gorbachev, former president of the Soviet Union, among others.

On October 16, 1992, Francis Sejersted, chairman of the Nobel committee, announced that Rigoberta Menchú Tum was being recognized for her work for social justice.

Rigoberta's story and that of thousands of other Mayan Quiché Indians had come to the attention of the Nobel committee as a result of her autobiography, *I Rigoberta Menchú, An Indian Woman in Guatemala,* which was published in 1983.

Rigoberta's remarkable story recounts the first 20 years of her life. It is a powerful and heart-rending tale told with simplicity and truth. Her story reveals the modern history of Guatemala and what it has been like for poor Guatemalans during this repressive and bloody period.

The brutality Rigoberta lived through transformed her from a shy young woman into a revolutionary for peace and justice. Her vision of a better life and a saner world grew out of the experiences in her village, her love of her family, the sadness of their loss, and the rich stories and heritage of her ancestors throughout 1,000 years of Mayan culture. The situation in Guatemala is similar to that of South Africa, where a white minority ruled over a black majority. In Guatemala Indians make up more than 55 percent of the population, and for centuries they have been locked out of power by the ruling white minority government.

During a dangerous civil war, Rigoberta chose to battle the Guatemalan government for the civil rights of Mayan Indians, the indigenous or native people of Guatemala. She was uneducated and poor, and she was armed only with her weapons of choice: words and her wits.

Like David fighting Goliath, she fought against all odds and won. She learned Spanish, the language of her oppressors, and used the government's own words to fight for her cause. Rigoberta used native Mayan dialects to convince other Indians that by banding together they could become a powerful voice for their common interests. And she used her wits to outsmart those who tried to brutalize her people.

Rigoberta Menchú Túm's story reflects the Mayan heritage of cruelty, exploitation, and repression, but her story is not all tragedy. She has a proud culture and she has experienced many happy and magical moments in her village.

Rigoberta's life is a lesson for all of us: Heroes are not born perfectly formed but can grow from the most humble beginnings. And if we want it badly enough, each of us can become a hero with the potential to change the world, becoming lights for the eyes of the next generation.

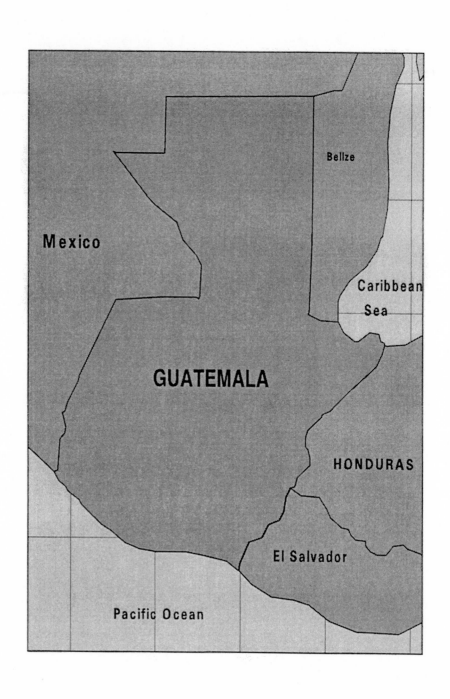

CHAPTER 1: CHIMEL

"Where I live is practically a paradise, the country is so beautiful."

Rigoberta's story begins in the garden paradise she calls home—Guatemala—a country about the size of the state of Ohio. Guatemala is located in Central America on that skinny stretch of land that looks like a piece of taffy pulled taut between the United States and South America. Guatemala lies just south of Mexico in a basin of the Caribbean sea between the Pacific Ocean and the Gulf of Honduras. Its neighbors are Belize, Honduras, and El Salvador.

Rigoberta was born on January 9, 1959, in the village of Chimel, located in the northwest province of El Quiché. The nearest large town is San Miguel Uspantan, the administrative center of El Quiché.

Uspantan is well know in Guatemala for its vivid and bloody history. In 1529, the well-prepared Uspanteca Indians and their Ixil allies defeated a young Spanish commander and his invading forces. At their victory party, the Indians tore out the Spaniards' hearts and offered them to war gods.

The following year, the Spaniards returned for revenge. This time, a more experienced commander led Spanish soldiers as they torched villages and slaughtered the Uspanteca Indians. Survivors were branded like cattle and sold into slavery.

But for young Rigoberta and her brothers and sisters, all that was ancient history—or so they thought. Like most of the Indians of Guatemala, Rigoberta spent her early

years in the altiplano, the central highlands of the Cuchu-
mantanes Mountains.

From an airplane the area looks like a series of dark
green cones with an occasional thin threadlike path con-
necting one village to another. There are no big roads
in the mountains, because there are no cars. Everyone
walks from village to village, and everything comes down
the mountainside by horseback or backpack.

Rigoberta grew up hearing the story of how her parents
came to settle Chimel. Vincent and Juana had grown up
poor but worked hard. When they were very young, they
fell in love, married, and built their first house. But earning
a living and supporting a family was so difficult that they
soon lost their home to creditors—local wealthy landowners.

In 1960, when Rigoberta was a year old, Juana and
Vincent made a decision to move to the mountains and
start again. They had grown up hearing Rigoberta's grand-
father tell stories of the beautiful Guatemalan countryside
that belonged to everyone. But when Vincent and Juana
selected their new home site and were ready to build their
house in the mountains, they discovered that things had
changed. The Guatemalan government now claimed own-
ership of all land and demanded that home builders pay a
fee before clearing the land.

Discouraged but not dissuaded, the Menchús scraped
together the fee and built their home. As more families
moved to the area, the Menchús helped the new arrivals
build homes and abide by government rules.

Vincent and Juana were well-respected in the growing
community and eventually were elected the first village
leaders. In addition to raising their own five children, the

Menchús took an active role in the community. In a Mayan village the whole community becomes the "children" of the elected leaders.

As village leader, Rigoberta's father Vincent carried out the people's wishes. He often presided over village business meetings during which important decisions were made. Sometimes villagers discussed who could volunteer to help a young family build their first house. At other Thursday–night meetings, villagers would talk about land problems with the government or they might select someone to accompany Vincent in his travels to the capital for talks with the government.

Rigoberta was proud of her father, but as his responsibilities increasingly took him away from home, she began to worry that something might happen to him.

While Vincent was away, the other Menchús were busy with life in Chimel. In the United States, we commonly encounter people of other cultures and religions, but in Chimel, everyone was the same—Mayan—and shared the same cultural beliefs and religion.

Corn or "maize" as Mayans call it, is the center of their lives. They eat it and they celebrate it in their stories and fiestas. When Rigoberta and her brothers and sisters were young, they listened to and learned the ancient Mayan stories of creation: The creator first made man from wood, but wood was too rigid. Then he tried clay, but it was too easily broken. Finally, he made a corn paste called "masa" from crushed, hulled kernels, and it was just right.

Planting corn is a sacred practice for the Mayans. Villagers gather a month before planting time for a ceremony in which they ask the earth's permission to plant the seeds. At the fiesta, villagers burn incense. Elected leaders, such as Vincent Menchú, say prayers. The whole community prays that the sun, the rain, and the animals will watch over the seeds and make sure they grow. Indians understand that only then will they have food to eat for the coming year. In return, the villagers promise not to waste water or any of their harvest.

The people of Chimel, like all Mayan Indians, have great respect for nature. They believe that the sun, earth, and water give them maize. Maize, in turn, is the means by which they are able to live. The villagers are thankful for that. In the Mayan tradition, the community joins together to help sow and harvest the fields of corn, called "milpas." If a woman is widowed or a farmer has been ill and unable to plant, other families help them cultivate their land and harvest their crops.

The land around Chimel is not particularly good for farming. It took eight years of hard work for the village to produce enough corn, beans, and squash to feed everyone. Rigoberta's family also had sheep, chickens, and a few dogs to scare wild animals away.

Juana especially loved animals and knew a lot about medicinal plants. She was able to teach her children how to understand and care for animals. The Menchú dogs never barked at Juana and never bit anyone in the family because, according to Rigoberta, her mother had such a special way with them.

Had Juana lived where there were other opportunities, she might have become a veterinarian. As a young girl, she studied with a "chiman," a Mayan priest or doctor. In Chimel, she was a midwife who attended almost every birth in the village. When anyone was sick or hurt, they turned to Juana for plants and herbal cures. She helped her family and friends overcome many natural enemies, but she was powerless to stop the man-made evils that would threatened her people.

As a little girl, Rigoberta remembers lying in the jungle and looking up into a canopy of leaves so thick that "not a single ray of light fell through the plants." No wonder Guatemala is the Mayan word for "land of many trees." Mighty rivers gushed down the mountainside below the Menchú home. And on those dark and dreamy star-filled nights, the mountain air was like an icy blast from an open freezer, bone-chillingly cold and damp.

When the sun came out, the jungle came alive with white orchids and sing-song birds, including the quetzal with its long, swooping, colorful tail. The quetzal is the national bird of Guatemala, renown for being unable to live in captivity.

If we were to visit Chimel, we could see the Menchú's tiny low-slung house. It is windy in the mountains, and a tall house could be carried away on a windy day. The average Mayan house takes about 15 days to build. All the materials come from the trees. No nails are used. The walls are made of straight sticks of cane stuck into the ground, preferably cane cut during a full moon. The Indians believe this cane is stronger and longer lasting. The houses are topped with a layer of large flat leaves fastened to the walls by natural fibers.

When Rigoberta was growing up, Chimel had no electricity. At night, the village would glow with the dancing flames of "ocote" pieces. When lit, these pine torches would ignite as if doused with gasoline. Rigoberta's whole family—mother, father, sisters, brothers, their wives, and children—all slept together on floor mats. They had no mattresses. Above them in a second-floor loft called the "tapanco," they stored the corn from their family plot.

An average day in the Menchú household began early. Juana always rose first and thanked the dawning day. Then she would start the fire to heat water—not for coffee, because the Menchús couldn't afford it—but for washing the "nixtamal"—a mixture of maize, corn, and lime, which Juana pounded and massaged into dough for her family's tortillas.

For centuries the Mayan have cooked in earthenware pots rather than in metal pans or ovens. This is how Juana taught Rigoberta to cook when she was old enough, just as she had been taught by her mother.

Mayan women grind the maize and lime mixture with a stone and fashion perfect paper-thin pancakes by passing the dough from one hand to the other. The tortillas are then cooked on flat earthenware pans on the open fire. Tortillas are an essential food for the Mayans; they eat meat only on special occasions, such as birthdays and weddings.

Throughout the village, everyone had a job to do. Children were expected to help out from a very early age. Rigoberta's first responsibilities were feeding the dogs and gathering sticks for the fire. When she was older, she helped weed the milpas.

The Menchú family's happiest times were spent in the mountains with the animals—even snakes—and the flowers and birds. Because their land could not grow enough to support them, the Menchú family lived high in the mountains for three or four months of the year and then traveled down the mountain to work on a "finca."

Fincas are big plantations. Most are located along

the fertile coast. The plantations grow many products for export: sugar, coffee, cotton, and spices, such as cardamom.

Rigoberta hated going to the finca. One year, when she was very young, she had to be carried kicking and screaming to the truck that would carry her family on the long journey to the coast. For Rigoberta, life on the finca represented all that was wrong with Guatemala.

CHAPTER 2: THE FINCA

*"I started thinking about my childhood, and I
came to the conclusion that I hadn't had a childhood at all."*

When Rigoberta was only eight years old, she learned
one of the hardest lessons of her life. The Menchús
had decided to work on a finca along the southern coast
of Guatemala. The family desperately needed the extra
money they would all work hard to earn there.

Rigoberta had gone to the fincas with her family from
the time she was small enough to be carried in a shawl
on her mother's back. The Menchús, along with many
other families, traveled down the mountain to board over-
crowded trucks for the long ride to the coffee, banana,
cotton, or sugar plantations.

The rugged tooth-rattling trip took two-and-a-half days.
Often as many as 40 people were crammed together with
everything they could carry on their backs: bedding, clothing, plates and cups, and the water bottles they would
carry into the sweltering fields each day. Because sometimes no family member remained in the village, even the
chickens, goats, and pigs were herded into the truck.

The trip was long, dark, and frightening. The truck ca-
reened down narrow mountain paths, bouncing and bang-
ing around hairpin turns. Pigs squealed, and children
cried. In all the years she traveled from Chimel to the
coast, Rigoberta never once got even a glimpse of the
beautiful countryside she was passing through. The man
who recruited workers was called "the caporales." He had
little regard for the workers. The caporales drove the truck
and rarely stopped to let anyone go to the bathroom or

stretch their legs. Children who couldn't wait any longer wet themselves and wailed as the truck rumbled through the mountains.

Rigoberta was especially sensitive to the smells. Although she tried to sleep, the constant jerking and bouncing, the clammy elbows and knees of strangers pressing in upon her, and the overwhelming pungent odor of so many people and animals crowded together made her sick. She pleaded with her mother, "Why must we go?"

In response, Juana caressed Rigoberta's cheek and shook her head in resignation, "Because we have to. When you're older you'll understand."

At two years old, Nicolas Menchú did not understand the journey either. Rigoberta's little brother was sick from the first day they arrived on the finca and cried endlessly for two weeks.

Rigoberta, her mother, sisters, and little brother lived in a "galera," a rustic house with many other families. They had no plumbing, no running water, no toilet, and no medical care.

Vincent and the boys went to another finca where their back-breaking work on the sugar cane plantation would earn the family a bit more money. Splitting families up for months at a time was common practice on the finca.

Juana worked in the fields every day and tried to care for her children. Even though she had always helped the sick in Chimel, nothing seemed to relieve Nicolas's illness. There was no clinic, no doctor, and no money for medicine. Most of the time there was not even enough food. And no extra food was ever provided for mothers breastfeeding their babies.

Nicolas, like most Indian children, was so malnourished

to begin with that he had difficulty fighting off any illness. Juana was fearful of losing her job, so she carried Nicolas sick as he was with her into the fields. She could not leave him behind even though she was terrified to bring him with her.

Juana had experienced first hand the dangers of bringing a small child into the fields. Before Nicolas was born, she lost baby Filipe when pesticides were sprayed on the crops as she stood with him in the fields.

On the fifteenth day, Nicholas's suffering ended and he too died. Juana was unconsolable. Most of the other Indians who worked and lived alongside the Menchús were from other villages and spoke different dialects. Juana could not even share her grief with her neighbors. She had no one to turn to for help.

When the finca boss found out about the baby's death, he told Juana that for a fee she could bury Nicolas on finca property. The thought of leaving him there was unbearable but she had no choice. As she grieved for her baby, Juana worked twice as hard to earn the money to bury her child.

Nicholas was laid to rest in a small suitcase-like box built by a neighbor. The next day the caporales told the family to leave the finca. He claimed they had missed too much work attending to the baby and demanded payment for the baby's burial and "medicines."

Juana knew that there had been no medicine for Nicolas, but when she protested, all he replied was, "Boss's orders." Desperate to return to Chimel, Juana borrowed the money from neighbors and promised to pay it back as soon as she could.

After the burial and with a great deal of sadness, Juana and her children set out for Chimel. Vincent Menchú did not even learn of his son's death until three weeks later when he returned from work on the other finca. As he struggled to come to terms with his son's death, he learned of the caporales's demand for money and the family's growing debts.

At the end of the month, villagers returned from the finca and told the Menchús how the caporales had left their names on the pay roster and collected all of their wages for himself.

Nicolas's death broke Rigoberta's heart. In addition to the anger and fear that would be with her forever, his death symbolized all that was wrong with life in Guatemala. She recalled the long, hot days and nights spent working in the fields—even small children—with never enough to eat; how ruthlessly the landowners treated their workers; the land policies that allowed the wealthy landowners who represented only 2 percent of Guatemalans to control 70 percent of the land; the lack of government regulations to protect workers; and staunch government support for whatever the finca owners wanted to do.

Little had changed since the Spanish first enslaved the Indians in the 1500's. The government had always seen to it that the Indians "needed" to work on the fincas. In the early days, Indians were simply forced to work for the Spanish. Later, the government confiscated Indian land and handed it over to those who would build Guatemala's coffee and mining industries. If the Indians revolted or complained about these policies, the government would punish them by taking more land.

Sometimes the land was sold cheaply to the large fincas or, worse, was left idle. By not allowing the Indians to plant their lands, the government, in effect, forced them to work on the fincas if they wanted to eat. The system of providing cheap workers for the labor-hungry fincas had been in place for generations. And it continued to churn out misery and pain for the current generation of Indians, including the Menchús.

CHAPTER 3: SCHOOL

"My children don't aspire to go to school, be-cause schools take our customs away from us."

Like most of the young Mayans, Rigoberta did not go to school. Vincent was dead set against it—not because he didn't want his children to read or write, but because he was suspicious of what his children would be taught at school and what they might lose of themselves and their culture in the process.

Chimel had no community school, but at nearby schools the children wore shoes and uniforms. Victor thought the schools were trying to make Indian children into something they were not. He had heard that the schools taught children that Pedro de Alvarado was a great Spanish hero and conquistador. For the Menchús and other Mayans, de Alvarado was the white man who in 1527 killed their beloved Quiché king, Tecum Uman. The Mayans knew de Alvarado as the man who began the exploitation of the Guatemalan Indians. He was not their hero.

Victor Menchú wanted his children to preserve their Mayan heritage, language, customs, traditions, and to revere their history. The Menchús were descendants of the Quiché branch of the Mayan culture. Rigoberta had heard stories of her ancestors for as long as she could remember. The stories made her proud of her ancestors. Almost daily, like a videotape playing in her head, she relived over and over again the most dramatic and historic Mayan dramas.

When Paris was a village, the Mayans had already developed a sophisticated culture in the jungles of southern Mexico, Belize, Guatemala, El Salvador, and Honduras.

Their civilization was rich in politics, art, architecture, and engineering. The Mayans were the first to use the mathematical concept of zero. They invented a calendar remarkably like our own, consisting of 366 days. They recorded eclipses and documented their knowledge of astronomy, which they used as a guide in planting their crops.

To the ancient Mayans, recording their history was important. Instead of writing books, they documented the lives of kings and recreated important cultural events by painting hieroglyphics, or pictures, on the walls of temples and by carving limestone statues.

The Mayan way of life had been threatened for generations by outsiders who wanted to control the Indians. When the Spanish first came, many of the Mayans died of smallpox and other diseases that the Europeans brought with them. Since then, outsiders had attempted to destroy the culture in an effort to dominate the people and the rich natural resources that surrounded them.

Vincent believed that schools were simply a means of breaking down the community and culture. He had been taken advantage of by outsiders before, and he would not trust them with something as important as his children's welfare.

Instead, Rigoberta got her education through experience. She learned economics by watching how money changed hands. Once when Rigoberta was in the capital with her father, she saw an automobile for the first time. She thought it was a slow-moving animal until her father explained that it was like the truck that had taken them to the finca, except that it was smaller and carried fewer people.

Although she did not personally ever know anyone who

owned a car, she learned on the finca that the wealthy owner could afford fancy Mercedes, BMW's, and Range Rovers, yet all he could pay the field workers was about $1.20 a day.

She learned about labor practices, too, as she watched how the plantation owners hired workers. The finca owner hired a caporales to recruit laborers. The caporales was usually a "ladino," a person of mixed Indian and Spanish heritage, or an Indian who had adopted Western ways.

The caporales generally spoke both an Indian dialect and Spanish. He served as the intermediary between the Indian laborer and plantation owner. He was given a truck with which to transport workers, and he was paid by the head for each worker he brought to the finca.

Caporales would go into the highlands and give money to the Indians for a contract to work during the coming harvest. The worker was required to work off the loan, plus high interest. For the Indians, the system was similar to using a credit card, but with exorbitant "interest" payments, often resulting in a lifetime of debt. The Indian literally sold his soul without knowing it. Rigoberta watched this system and came to understand what discrimination and exploitation meant.

Even when workers realized what was happening, not speaking or understanding Spanish made it difficult for them to argue their cases. The caporales made it clear that he believed the workers were ignorant, lazy, dirty, and inferior—even though they were the direct descendants of the proud original people of Guatemala.

Those lucky enough to survive the trip to the finca could be sure that life there would be worse than the journey. The caporales, who frequently became the finca boss, would be a tireless taskmaster in the fields, constantly pushing them to work faster and harder.

Families routinely were split up for months at a time, with the men going off to work the sugar cane plantations, which paid a higher wage, while the women and children remained behind to do less lucrative work.

The Menchús, like all Indians on the finca, lived in a "galera," or large shack with a banana or palm frond roof without walls or room dividers, toilet, or running water. Sometimes 400 to 500 people and their animals were crammed into these houses. For seven long months, the family lived in these miserable and unsanitary conditions.

The "galera" as it was called often housed a diverse group of people from the 23 ethnic groups in Guatemala, all speaking different dialects and thus unable to communicate with each other. Only their "friend," the caporales, could serve as their intermediary.

Rigoberta often wanted to make friends with the other children. They had so much in common, but they couldn't understand each other. Surrounded and yet isolated in a sea of 500 faces, Rigoberta began to see that her family was not alone in their suffering. Many people from different regions shared their pain.

At age eight, Rigoberta went to work on a coffee plantation. At age 10, she picked cotton in the hot sun on the far southern coast. After her first day in the cotton fields, she awakened in the middle of the night and lit a candle. A mask of mosquitoes covered the faces of her sleeping brothers and sisters. On their eyes and in their mouths, the hungry insects feasted. In horror, she reached up to touch her own face, only to find that it too was covered with mosquitoes.

For the rest of the night, she was haunted by the image of mosquitos eating her alive. It was hard to dream about a better life or to be optimistic about the future. She had no hope that anything would ever change. The finca owners would continue to make huge profits, and the caporales would be well rewarded. Neither one would ever care about the workers who made them both rich.

Rigoberta learned about politics on the finca. Once on the cotton plantation, the overseer called the workers together for an address by the landowner. The landowner wanted to thank the workers for their labor. Rigoberta had never seen such a huge fat man. Even his fancy leather shoes fascinated and yet repulsed her. She had never seen anything like them. Most Indians were barefoot. Those who could afford shoes wore "caitios," a simple leather sandal with a rubber sole.

A group of armed soldiers accompanied the landowner. Rigoberta asked her mother why the soldiers were forcing the landowner to speak to them. Her mother explained that the soldiers were the landowner's bodyguards. People who are afraid need protection, her mother explained.

The landowner told the workers about an upcoming presidential election. He instructed them to vote for "their" president by marking an X on the ballot beside a particular name. The overseer explained that anyone who did not vote properly would be thrown off the finca without pay.

Later, the landowner met with the workers again to congratulate them on their new president. Juana and Vincent laughed at the mention of "their president." This was Rigoberta's first exposure to government, but she knew that this government did not represent her.

Everyone on the finca had a job. When Rigoberta was

only five, her mother's job was to cook for 40 workers. Rigoberta's job was to look after her little brother. Juana would begin meal preparation at 3 a.m. and then work until 7 p.m. picking coffee to supplement her earnings. She knew how difficult the field work was and tried to provide fresh nourishing food for the workers, even though her ingredients often were of poor quality. Rigoberta saw how hard her mother worked and felt useless and weak because she was too young to help.

Food was a major concern for every family on the finca. Generally, there was never enough of it because the landowner allotted food for only those who worked. Families were forced to stretch their meager meals to feed children too young to work and the elderly. For these Indians it wasn't a matter of finding something they liked to eat; they ate whatever they could get their hands on.

When she was eight, Rigoberta started earning money, 20 centavos (cents) a day for picking 35 pounds of coffee. The Menchús trained their children to delicately pluck the beans from the coffee plants. Little hands could pick the beans without breaking the young branches. The children also were most agile at running their fingers over already picked plants looking for missed beans. This "second picking" was among the most difficult work on the plantation, but it paid no more than any other.

The overseer watched for damage to the plants and charged the workers for broken branches. Rigoberta disciplined herself and over time increased her picking quota by a pound a day. Some days, because of the hot sun and headaches from the pesticides, she needed help from her brothers and sisters to meet her goal. But on most days, she was determined to reach her goal alone.

By the time she was 10, Rigoberta earned a raise for picking 40 pounds of coffee a day. Undermining her efforts, however, was the politics of the plantation. Sometimes the overseer would steal a few pounds from the workers' harvests or tamper with the scales. Whatever he could claim for himself was that much less he would have to pay to the workers. Rigoberta learned important lessons from these endless everyday injustices.

For Juana, the worst times were when one of her children was ill. Sickness was a constant worry as the family endured the dramatic climate change in moving from the mountains to the coast. In addition, the Menchús—especially the children—constantly were subjected to infections that resulted from 400 to 500 people living so closely together in very unsanitary conditions.

The finca provided an outlet for the workers' worries and frustration: the cantina. In the "cantina," or bar, parents could drink alcohol to escape their insurmountable troubles. More than once, Rigoberta watched her father spend too much time in the cantina. It was actually possible for a worker to drown his troubles in alcohol and lose an entire week's wages in one evening. The finca bosses had every possible angle covered.

At 14, Rigoberta suffered another painful loss. She and her best friend Maria were picking cotton together when the fields were sprayed with pesticide. Maria died from the poison. Rigoberta hated those responsible for the spraying and blamed them for Maria's death. With all the death and suffering she had seen in her young life, she began to wonder what this struggle called life was all about. She thought she knew all there was to know about sadness, but she had many more lessons ahead.

CHAPTER 4: DREAMS

"I'd always seen my mother cry.... I was afraid of life and asked myself, what will it be like when I'm grown up?"

Like all young girls, Rigoberta often wondered what her future would hold. Would she marry and have many children? What would they look like, and where would they live? Who would she marry? Would they live in the mountains and travel to the finca as her parents had?

When Rigoberta was 10 years old, she got what many girls her age only dream about.It wasn't a bicycle or a new dress, not even a room of her own. Instead, she received something she could treasure long after a bike would rust or a dress would fall to pieces.

On her tenth birthday, Rigoberta was given a special gift as well as a peek into the future. The scene was carefully orchestrated by Rigoberta's parents, her older brothers, and her sister. They gathered with pride to celebrate Rigoberta's young life and to tell her about her future. It was the traditional rite-of-passage ceremony to which all young Mayans look forward.

Her parents, Vincent and Juana, began the solemn ceremony by thanking Rigoberta for being their devoted child and for the money she had earned and the hard work she had undertaken on behalf of her family. The Menchús gathered around Rigoberta and told her that life as an adult would be difficult and that she would always be poor. They warned her that she would never realize many of her dreams, but they promised that she would find happiness and fulfillment through her family's love.

As Rigoberta listened, her heart pounded and her mind raced with excitement and apprehension. Her family urged her not to be sad or bitter about the difficulties that lay ahead. Her mother talked about menstruation, a physical change in Rigoberta's body that would one day lead to babies and motherhood. Rigoberta was at once entranced with the possibilities and yet relieved to know that her mother would be there to answer her questions.

Flushing with sisterly pride, Rigoberta's older sister recalled what she had been like at age 10, 12, 13, and 15. She reminded Rigoberta how much she had already learned and then cautioned about important Mayan traditions: From this day forward Rigoberta must stay close to her mother during fiestas. She was never to cut her hair, wear makeup, or in any way tamper with her natural beauty.

Rigoberta's parents presented her with two "cortes," the multicolored fabric Guatemalan women wear as a skirt and two "perrajes," or cotton cloaks. Rigoberta had already learned to weave and could make a "huipil" (pronounced weepel), the loose-fitting embroidered or woven Mayan blouse. From now on Rigoberta would be a respected young woman in the community and she would dress the part.

Traditional Mayan weaving dates back to ancient times. Through dreams, Mayan women find inspiration for the bright fucias, blues, greens, and yellows in their weaving. The colors and patterns reflect the spirit or force of the women's ancestors and their culture or village. The embroidery on a man's shirt may tell whether he is married and how many children he has.

Rigoberta's father Vincent went on to explain that with

her new freedoms came serious responsibilities. Within a few days Rigoberta would be formally initiated into the adult community. The eyes of the entire village would be on her. In return for their love, confidence, and protection, Rigoberta would be expected to set a good example for young children. She must never do anything to dishonor herself or her ancestors.

Days later at the formal initiation, Rigoberta was asked what kind of community work she would do. She chose to follow in her father's footsteps and become a catechist. She would teach children in the village and on the finca Bible stories and Catholic customs.

Rigoberta's father Vincent was a devout Catholic, an altar boy. He taught Rigoberta many Bible stories and how the Spanish conquerors brought Catholicism to Guatemala. The Spanish had hoped that by converting the Indians to Catholicism they could also gain control of Mayan villages.

In spite of the Spaniards' questionable motives, the Indians identified with Catholicism because they saw many similarities between the Catholic religion and their own Mayan traditions. Both worship one god. Catholics believe in Jesus, and the Mayans believe in the Sun god. The Mayans set out to lead a good life by imitating the lives of their ancestors, and Catholics pattern their lives after the saints. Both Mayans and Catholics believe strongly in an afterlife. And both groups have endured the persecution, suffering, and death of a great figure. For Catholics, it is the crucifixion of Jesus, and for the Mayans, the torture and death of Quiché prince Tecum Uman who was murdered by Spanish conquerors.

Even their religious ceremonies are similar: Catholics use music, incense, and processions, whereas the Mayans use music and fiestas and burn copal, a resin from trees that smells like incense. In fact, today it is possible to see Guatemalan Indians burning incense on the steps of the church to honor saints and gods before going in for Catholic services.

During Vincent's life there were not many priests in the highlands, and the Mayans blended the two religions to suit themselves. During Rigoberta's early years, priests from other countries, such as Canada and the United States, came to Guatemala to spread their religion, but they also saw injustices and tried to help the Indians overcome them. These priests influenced Rigoberta in many ways.

On Rigoberta's special initiation day, she faced the whole village and repeated for herself the promises that Vincent and Juana had made to the community when she was born. In a prayerful ceremony, Rigoberta acknowledged that she belonged to the community and was ready to contribute to the common good. She announced that she would become a catechist and take over some of her father's responsibilities, such as visiting and praying for the sick. She would spend the next year or so perfecting her skills, memorizing Bible stories, and working with the children.

During her initiation, Rigoberta discovered her "nahual," which is a shadow or protective spirit. The Mayans believe that every child is born with a representative on earth through which the child communicates with nature. The identity of the nahual must not be revealed outside of the community.

Rigoberta's formal initiation ceremony ended with a special gift from her parents—a pig. This gift from Mayan parents to their children is designed to teach responsibility. Each child is totally responsible for the animal's survival. Every day of the pig's life, Rigoberta alone had to decide what to feed it and how to afford the food. No one could sell her pig or touch it without her permission. If, for example, Rigoberta decided to breed the pig, she would then have had to plan for the care of the piglets or she might sell the piglets to buy food for the mother, who in turn could breed again. Rigoberta had to devise a plan and execute it in addition to her other duties in the family and the community.

Rigoberta chose to plant and care for an extra plot of maize to support her pig. Like her mother, she loved animals, so raising the pig was not difficult for her.

Childhood had officially ended for Rigoberta. She was enthusiastic about her new freedoms and her new adventures. That same year, she begged her father to go to Guatemala City to work as a maid. Even though her sister had hated the work and returned home, Rigoberta dreamed of mastering Spanish and learning to read. She believed that working as a maid couldn't be any worse than working on the fincas or at home. She was determined to go and always ready to work hard.

Later that year, the finca owner asked Vincent to let Rigoberta work as his family's maid in Guatemala City. Vincent reluctantly agreed. Rigoberta was thrilled. Finally, she would journey to Guatemala City with the landowner and his armed guards in tow. She was excited and told herself, "I must be brave..." She was almost 13, and she was exhilarated and yet terrified about what lay ahead.

CHAPTER 5: THE MAID

"Indians are lazy. They don't work, that's why they're poor. "

Bouncing along in the back of the truck, Rigoberta was exhausted but too excited to sleep. Her heart raced as she tried to imagine what lay ahead. She knew that working for the finca boss would be difficult, but she hoped that the loneliness and isolation would pay off in other ways. She wanted desperately to learn Spanish and know a bit more about the ways of the world. When she arrived in Guatemala City, she found not only a demanding mistress and three sons—ages 22, 15, and 12—but a household that made her feel worthless and alone.

When Rigoberta stepped into the house for the first time, her limited Spanish didn't prevent her from understanding exactly what her new mistress thought as she recoiled at the sight of Rigoberta's soiled work clothes. Her mistress ordered Candalaria, the other house maid, to get Rigoberta out of the kitchen immediately. She was ushered to a back storage room littered with boxes, plastic bags, and other trash. A tiny soiled bed with a mat and a small blanket lay buried beneath the mess.

It was here that Rigoberta would spend many a sleepless night and here that she ate her first dinner of beans and hard tortillas—alone. She was hungry, but the food stuck in her throat because she had never before felt so alone and unwelcome.

Rigoberta wondered how long she could last in this house. But she refused to give up. As the days passed, she noticed that Candelaria, a Mayan who wore ladino clothes and spoke Spanish, was entrusted with the household cooking and shopping. Candelaria was a servant but she also ran the household with a strange and powerful authority. Rigoberta, on the other hand, was only allowed to do the most menial chores. Even the family dog got better treatment and better food. He ate the leftover scraps of meat and rice from the dinner table, and Rigoberta got what a dog wouldn't eat.

On one of her first mornings in the new household, Rigoberta started her day by washing the breakfast dishes. But when her mistress noticed that she still had no clean clothes, she was furious. She screamed at Candelaria, "How filthy! Get that girl out of here! Don't let her touch the dishes. Can't you see how dirty she is?"

Rigoberta spent the rest of the day tightly clutching a broom handle as she swept every inch of the yard and watered the plants. Later, her mistress summoned her. "I am ashamed for my friends to see you at the market," she said. I won't have you in my house in those filthy things. I will advance you two months' pay to buy new clothes.

Rigoberta was already in debt—15 quetzals (or $15)—to her mistress for a new huipil and corte. With her next check, three months later, she would be expected to buy shoes. She felt herself sinking further into the debt and servitude that had trapped her people for hundreds of years.

Time stood still for Rigoberta. Her life consisted of piles of dirty dishes and mountains of laundry and ironing followed by endless dusting and sweeping. But the mind-numbing work wasn't the worst part. Rigoberta had never before felt so humiliated. Her face burned with shame every time she looked into her mistress's eyes and saw her own reflection as a lazy, worthless Indian.

Not a day passed that Rigoberta's mistress didn't complain bitterly about her work and call her names. Rigoberta spent countless hours remaking tidy beds and rewashing clean dishes. Her only relief came when the master and his sons screamed for her to fetch their slippers and bring their meals. The days of drudgery droned on with little relief.

Two long months later, her worst fear came to pass: A father's visit should have been a joyous occasion, but Rigoberta dreaded Vincent's coming. She loved her father too much to see him subjected to the humiliation she lived with every day.

Vincent Menchú had come to the capital on village business and had been traveling for many days. The government frequently sent him from one city to the next to sign papers. They hoped that if they kept him busy he would lose interest in organizing effective Indian resistance to unfair government policies. He arrived dirty and tired from his travels. He had run out of money and was humiliated to have to ask his daughter for a loan to get him home.

Rigoberta's mistress did not see a man in distress; she saw a "filthy Indian." She told Rigoberta to go into the street to see her father and not to bring him into her house. Rigoberta greeted her father warmly and explained that he was not welcome in the house. Tearfully, she told him that she had no money because she was already in debt for new clothing.

Rigoberta confided her troubles in Candelaria, who spoke fluent Spanish. She, in turn, demanded the money from their mistress. Rigoberta was pleased but puzzled by Candelaria's power.

The mistress threw ten quetzals in Rigoberta's face and yelled that incompetent maids were always trying to steal her food and take her money. This was one time Rigoberta gladly endured the abuse. She handed the money to her father, kissed him, and wished him a safe trip home.

Little by little, Rigoberta could understand more Spanish, but with no instruction she still could not speak it. Even so, she was proud of how much she had learned. Every day she was better able to communicate with Candelaria, who cautioned her not to let the mistress push her around. Candelaria warned Rigoberta that the more subservient she was, the more abusive her mistress would become.

Candelaria told Rigoberta of her plans to quit her job. The mistress had been pressuring her to "teach" her sons about sex. When she refused, the mistress became angry. The situation came to a head around Christmas when the family was preparing to celebrate the holidays. Rigoberta and Candelaria had to make 200 tamales and kill, dress, and cook four turkeys.

Candelaria had a plan. She and Rigoberta would kill the turkeys and then demand two extra days off during the holidays. If the mistress refused, they would leave her to cook her own turkeys or let them rot. Rigoberta was fearful of losing her pay, and was incapable of disobedience. When the mistress discovered Candelaria's plan, she threw her out two days before Christmas, leaving Rigoberta to do all the work.

Rigoberta worked feverishly to prepare the 200 tamales and cook the turkeys. While she cleaned the house and china for the festivities, washing and ironing piled up. On Christmas day, the family and guests got drunk and at midnight they sent Rigoberta out for more wine. Because she was unfamiliar with the area, she returned home empty handed.

Her mistress humiliated Rigoberta in front of the guests. Rather than coming to her defense, the others at the party complained bitterly about their own Indian servants. "Indians are all alike. They are lazy; they don't want to work. That's why they're poor. They're always making trouble because they won't work."

Rigoberta was tired, hungry, angry, and so alone. From her room, she listened to the party chatter and gift giving, knowing full well that her only gift would be mountains of unwashed dishes. To her surprise, her mistress appeared in her doorway with a leftover tamale. Rigoberta's heart brightened at the small gesture of kindness. But just as she was about to savor the tamale, her mistress returned to retrieve it for an unexpected guest who had arrived late.

On the day after Christmas, Rigoberta was expected to clean up the holiday mess and do Candelaria's shopping and cooking. Rigoberta did not know her way around the city and had never before ventured out on her own. Upon hearing this, her mistress flew into a rage.

Rigoberta knew that she could not deal with this situation much longer. She would quit her job and return home to her parents as soon as she had a little money. For the next month, Rigoberta worked alone in the house. When she announced her resignation, she was dumbfounded to hear her mistress say, "We're so fond of you here. You must stay. I'll put your wages up, if you like."

Rigoberta was flattered but determined to go—especially

when her brother arrived with devastating news that their
father had been arrested.

CHAPTER 6: ENEMIES

*"Children, look after yourselves, because if I
don't come back you have to continue my work."*

Rigoberta was never sure about the source of her family's troubles. She knew they had problems and that sometimes creatures came in the night and stole things. She also knew that no matter how hard she and her brothers and sisters and parents worked, they were always poor and they never had enough to eat.

Rigoberta desperately wanted to confront "the enemy." She got her chance in 1975, when she was jolted to action by her father's arrest. Vincent was charged with "compromising the sovereignty of the state" and sentenced to 18 years in prison.

Rigoberta had no idea what the charges meant and she was terrified about losing her father. She and her brothers and sisters threw themselves into their work on the finca to earn money for the lawyers, translators, court fees, and bribes needed to free Vincent. During the 14 months he spent in a local jail, the family went without even the barest essentials.

Rigoberta's mother, Juana, worked as a maid in Santa Cruz del Quiché to be near the jail and the courts. Everyone in Chimel, who could, helped the Menchús raise money for Vincent's release. Rigoberta's brother traveled from the finca to the altiplano once a month to give money to Juana, who in turn traveled again and again to the courts. Travel to the prison was difficult, so rather than spend money visiting Victor, the family concentrated their energies on hiring educated people to help him. They knew that if he was sent from the local jail to the state prison, he would be there for the full 18 years. They had to free him before that happened.

Rigoberta always knew about Vincent's long struggle to protect village lands from seizure by the wealthy landowners. What she was now learning was how hard it was to fight a government that had a long history of siding with the landowners against the Indians. The only genuine effort at land reform had been a long time ago when peasants were encouraged to homestead vacant land. Even then, when the Indians worked hard for years, they often faced government seizure of their land when crop failures prevented them from making a profit and paying their debts. Even farmers who made money were sometimes forced to give up their land if wealthy landowners wanted it.

Three sets of landowners had caused the Menchús trouble during Rigoberta's life. First, were the Garcias, then the Martinezes, and currently the Brols—who wanted Chimel's land and prompted the police to arrest Vincent. All of these families owned large fincas. But no matter how much land they had, it was never enough. Whether they wanted land or workers, these families felt they were entitled to whatever they wanted, and their wealth gave them the means to accomplish almost anything.

In 1975, the Garcias had a produce market near Rigoberta's home. They also owned a nearby coffee finca where the Menchús sometimes worked instead of traveling to the coast. Rigoberta's friend, Petrona Chona, lived on the Garcia finca with her husband and two small children. The Chonas were miserably poor. Instead of wages, they worked to pay rent on a tiny house owned by the Garcias.

Carlos Garcia, the son of the landowner, was attracted to Petrona, who was very young and pretty. She ignored his flirting and made it clear that she was married and was not interested in him. Carlos was insistent and began to threaten her. One Friday, Petrona stayed home to care for her son who was ill. When he did not find her in the fields, Carlos went to the house and began harassing her. Neighbors heard them argue, and Carlos left in a rage.

Later, workers in the fields saw the Garcias' bodyguard come to the Chona house and heard Petrona scream. Upon Carlos's orders, the bodyguard had hacked Petrona to death with a machete while she carried her baby on her back. In the brutal attack, one of the baby's tiny fingers was severed from his hand. The workers who heard her screams had been afraid to get involved even when they saw the bodyguard arrive. They knew from experience that the landowner could do whatever he wanted.

Rigoberta had never before seen or touched a dead body. On the afternoon of the murder, Vincent and Rigoberta bandaged the baby's hand and stayed with Petrona's body. The workers were afraid to move her body at first for fear of being accused of the crime. By Sunday, no one had come to investigate the murder, so Vincent decided it was up to them to take care of the situation. Rigoberta helped Vincent and other neighbors collect Petrona's decomposing body and prepare it for burial

On Monday, the authorities arrived to investigate the crime. They stood laughing and talking with the Garcias for a long time. None of the witnesses were questioned. Finally, the bodyguard was arrested, and the Indians were encouraged. Their hope was short-lived: He was released after only 15 days in jail and returned to work almost immediately.

The struggle over land continued. Empowered by the

government's lack of interest in protecting the Indians, the landowners intensified their pressure on villagers to give up their lands. They even raided villages in an effort to scare Indians into leaving.

Years later, Rigoberta remembered, in particular, the graphic 1967 struggle between landowners and Indians. She was only eight years old and was terrified at the sight of Garcia's henchmen, whom she called the "finca soldiers." They rousted everyone out of their houses and ransacked their homes, breaking sacred cooking dishes and stealing keepsakes. Juana's precious silver necklace, which had been a gift from her mother, was stolen. Animals were killed, and the huts were destroyed.

For several days after the raid, it rained nonstop. The villagers were left with no protection. Indians from neighboring villages came to the rescue with new cooking pots, maize, and help in salvaging the few belongings that remained.

After many years of hard work, the Chimel harvests began to increase. Although each Indian family's plot was small, together their lands were sizeable enough to be coveted by wealthy landowners. As village leader, Vincent petitioned the government for help.

Vincent's land reform work often took him away from home. But when he returned, his neighbors would gather to hear his report about what had happened. Often Vincent would have to turn around the next day and return for more meetings in the capital.

Vincent made many trips to Guatemala City and met with the Guatemalan Institute for Agrarian Transformation (INTA). Government representatives repeatedly told Vincent not to worry about land titles. They advised him to tell the Indians to clear the undergrowth, measure and work the land because it belonged to them.

Vincent, in turn, reassured the villagers that their problems were over for now. At one point, INTA even gave the village a piece of paper, which according to the government confirmed title to the land. This was such an exciting development. Rigoberta remembered that she and all the children had signed it in ink with their fingertips.

Two years later, the landowners sent engineers to measure the land and inform the farmers that by signing that document they had given away their land rights. Vincent could not read Spanish and did not know what they had actually signed. He had trusted the government, and his trust had been betrayed.

Vincent was convinced that he had let the village down. The landowners' bribes were always more powerful than his quests for fair treatment. The Indians were victims of racism and their own poverty and illiteracy. They were vulnerable in negotiations with lawyers, landowners, and the government because they did not speak Spanish. They had less money for lawyers than their opponents and they were forced to hire interpreters who often were bribed to help the wealthy landowners get their way.

The landowners had the money and muscle to do whatever they wanted. They knew how to use the judges and the justice system to accomplish their goals legally. The powerful landowners even convinced themselves that what they were doing was right and just because their class and status entitled them to control and manage the "ignorant Indians."

Vincent sought help. He petitioned the Guatemalan Federation of Independent Unions for support. The farmers were, after all, agricultural laborers. The federation was convinced that Vincent had been deceived in the agreement, and they denounced government efforts to remove the Indians from their lands. At last, Vincent reasoned, the unions could take care of some of his affairs in the capital. He finally had some help. Ironically, this was the "crime" that would lead to his arrest.

The landowners were furious that the union support interfered with their control of the villagers. They reasoned that if they got rid of Vincent, the village would lack leadership and the landowners could regain control. They did not understand that Vincent was the elected leader who carried out village wishes. Even Rigoberta knew her father's role, because he often told his children,"Look after yourselves, because if I don't come back, you will have to continue my work...or we will lose our land."

Rigoberta began to understand what was happening to her family and to other peasant families. She saw language as a major obstacle for her people. Because many Indians spoke different dialects, often they could not communicate among themselves, much less understand government documents written in Spanish. Rigoberta made up her mind to learn Spanish from the nuns and priests in the area. She also decided to explore a little of her world by traveling to other villages as a catechist.

In her travels, Rigoberta saw that it was the work of the peasants that made the landowners wealthy. She knew from her months as a maid that the landowners saw the peasants only as strong arms to do their work, never as men and women. Her travels reinforced what she had long understood: that no matter how hard the Indians worked, they would never have enough food, clothing, or money, and their children would continue to die of malnutrition and disease. Something was terribly wrong.

Rigoberta visited her father in Santa Cruz del Quiché prison only once. It was a disturbing place. She saw prisoners who had fleas and diseases. Some were mad. Others constantly fought among themselves, hitting and biting each other. Rigoberta began to understand how courageous her father was.

Upon his release from jail, Vincent Menchú met with the community. He was happy, energized, and more determined than ever to fight for his village. Our ancestors were never cowardly, he said. "Prison is a punishment for the poor, but it doesn't eat people." Rigoberta did not understand what he meant. How could his time in jail have made him more focused on his work? His life in prison had been a horrible nightmare.

Upon Vincent's release, the community made several decisions. Families would not go to the fincas and leave their homes vulnerable to raids. Someone always would remain behind to guard the houses. Villagers trained their dogs to attack anyone who tried to enter their homes at night. Children learned how to keep watch and warn neighbors when they saw the landowners or government agents coming. The villagers had come to realize that their strength came from unity. They would organize to protect their homes or die trying.

During this time, the villagers lived very simple lives, in large part, because they did not have the means to do otherwise. Vincent traveled for three months, mostly in hiding and never alone. He was constantly being threatened by the landowners' hired gunmen who were angry at his release. Rigoberta and her family were now in danger too because they supported his efforts. They loved their father and knew that his work was important.

Rigoberta understood early on that her father could be shot or kidnapped or taken away from her. Although she did not want to think about such a horrible possibility, she knew that no matter what happened, her father's work must continue. "I'm your father now, but afterwards the community will be your father," he often told them.

The landowners were relentless, and Vincent knew that it was only a matter of time before he would be arrested again.

CHAPTER 7: CLIMATE OF UNREST

"What would it be like if all the Indians rose up and took the lands and the crops away from the landowners? Would they get weapons and kill us?"

Although Rigoberta was a teenager in the 1970's, according to Mayan traditions, she had been a woman for nearly six years. It was with a young woman's heart that she tried to understand the events that were tearing her family apart.

Just three weeks after her father was released from prison, he was kidnapped at gunpoint. The community had been aware of threats on Vincent's life. In response, village leaders insisted that he never travel alone. His companion was helpless, however, when the landowner's henchmen appeared out of nowhere and dragged Vincent off into the jungle.

The whole village organized a search. After a few hours, Vincent was found badly beaten. He was unable to walk and had to be carried to the hospital. This time his recovery took nine months, much of which he spent in hiding.

Then the unthinkable happened. In 1977, Vincent was arrested again and sentenced to life in prison for attempting to overthrow the government. Although his land-reform efforts had generated the support of his neighbors, labor unions, the federation of independent unions, priests, and nuns, it also had angered some powerful enemies. Vincent had become well-known in the region, and the Indian community clenched its fist in protest over his arrest.

This time, Vincent was released after 15 days in jail. His attackers made it clear, however, that he would never be safe, even in hiding. If he continued his work, they threatened to find him and kill him. If he could not be found, they would kill one of his children instead.

Land reform was such a fearful concept in Guatemala that some people could justify nearly any means to keep things from changing. Vincent Menchú became a lightening rod for the fears of a few powerful people who worried that if the Indians had their own lands, finca owners could not depend on cheap Indian labor to harvest their crops and guarantee their profits. Wealthy landowners were not about to give up their prosperity and way of life without a fight.

Change was not new to Guatemala, but it generally came slowly. Priests, nuns, and other religious workers had come to Guatemala from Spain, Canada, and the United States to work with the Indians in the 1940's and 1950's. They set out to encourage the Indians to develop a Christian acceptance of their plight on earth with the promise of reaping a better afterlife. While the church preached a spirit of passivity to the Indians, it encouraged wealthy landowners to be more charitable toward their workers.

In the 1960's and early 1970's, more priests and nuns came to Guatemala to save souls. These clerics soon understood that first they had to help the Indians overcome poverty and discrimination. These religious workers taught the Mayans to read and write and helped them organize cooperatives to market their handicrafts, weaving, and community crops. Each villager had a role in the cooperatives. Villagers who did not weave, might transport handicrafts or sell them at the market. Profits were divided equally among all workers, but often the profits were only enough to pay for supplies for the next religious holiday.

Learning to read and work together in the cooperative created an even stronger sense of community among the Indians. The cooperatives gave the Mayans hope for a better future. Although cooperatives were not designed to threaten the economic structure of the country, the government and landowners were afraid of any attempt to organize the Indians. They feared that a successful cooperative could undermine the balance of power that gave the landowners money, land, and political power and left the largest segment of the population, the Indians, with nothing.

In the early 1960's, a Spanish priest helped some of the Quiché Indians start a large and effective cooperative. The local merchants were the first to cry foul. They were angry because they were now forced to compete with the cooperative for customers. The cooperative's success reduced their profits.

The merchants petitioned the bishop to do something. He responded to their concerns by transferring the priest to another country. In other instances, community leaders were mysteriously kidnapped in an effort to scare Indians away from the cooperatives.

In time, the military began to openly attack the Indians. One by one, local Indian or cooperative leaders, priests, and nuns were kidnapped and murdered. News of the deaths spread quietly from one Mayan household to another. The rest of the world hardly noticed. No American or European newspapers printed the stories of village organizers who turned up missing and were later found dead in the remote highlands of Guatemala.

Most landowners and the military believed that the Indians were inferior, and that belief made it easier to torture and kill them. Left unchecked, the brutality and murders escalated. In the department of El Quiché, 168 cooperative and village leaders were killed between 1976 and 1978. The Indians and the religious workers knew what was happening, and each violent act increased their opposition to the government. Instead of gaining control, government-sponsored violence forced the Indians to support the only organization that seemed to have their interests at heart, the Guerrilla Army of the Poor (EGP).

Every time an Indian leader was murdered, the EGP gained strength. The Guerrilla Army of the Poor consisted of a small group of rebels who had survived battles with the military dating back to the early 1960's. They had not given up their hope of a Guatemalan revolution that would bring about reform at every level of society. But they understood that to succeed at this time, they needed the Indians' support. The EGP had been hiding in the jungle for years, planning and waiting for the right time. In the early 1970's, "the right time" finally arrived.

One of the first public acts of the Guerrilla Army of the Poor was to address the actions of Luis Arenas Barrera, a greedy landowner who monopolized land on the edge of the jungle in the Cuchumatanes mountains. Barrera paid the peasants very little and made sure that most of their wages came back to him as rent and payment for groceries. He charged the Indians high prices for a roof over their heads and half-full stomachs while they worked his land.

Barrera and his family lived very well in a large, well-guarded house. The guerrillas killed Arenas Barrera one payday in front of many workers. Word soon spread that the guerrillas had come to teach the landowners a lesson for getting rich at their workers' expense.

Meanwhile, Vincent was learning a different kind of lesson. In prison for the second time, he met a political prisoner who had defended peasants' rights and had a political vision for Guatemala. The man suggested that all the peasant farmers should form a league, a union of sorts, and unite to reclaim their lands. Vincent spent hours talking to this man. They discussed Guatemalan history and concluded that theirs was not a struggle between Indians and landowners but a revolution against a Guatemalan system that gave power and land only to a few.

Vincent would later tell the Mayans that they must use their heads for more than wearing their traditional hats. He encouraged them to think about what was happening and what they could do about it. After his release from prison, Vincent met with other peasants to set up the Committee of United Campesinos (CUC). From then on, Vincent remained in hiding. He lived an underground life, organizing for the CUC and living apart from his family for their safety.

As Rigoberta's Spanish improved, she began to travel to other communities. She felt connected to other villages and the common problems they shared. But the more she traveled, the more disturbed she became by the racism that existed between the Indians and poor ladinos. In a small village in Uspantan, Rigoberta listened as one of the nuns asked a little boy if his family were poor. He replied yes they were poor, but they were not Indians. Although he was as poor as any Indian, he had been taught to feel superior to them. It always puzzled Rigoberta why

Indian ways were shunned and their dress and customs considered inferior.

Language was a barrier that divided the Indians, and Rigoberta set out to cross that barrier. She knew Quiché and began to learn the two other main Mayan dialects: Mam and Cakchiquel. From these sprang the 22 ethnic dialects of Guatemala. In village after village, Rigoberta taught Bible stories to the children and self-defense skills to their elders. Self-defense was essential in light of ongoing military raids that made village security a top priority. The cooperatives could not be expanded until the villages were safe.

In her father's absence, Rigoberta was playing a more visible role in her community. As her village finalized its plans for self-defense, Rigoberta readied herself to step into her father's shoes and help protect her people from the monsters who came in the night.

CHAPTER 8: THE BATTLE

"Our main weapon is the Bible."

Trouble soon developed in the nearby village of San Pablo. One day the elected representatives and chief catechists of San Pablo and their families were kidnapped and never seen again. Although the villagers had begun to organize against a local landowner, they were not prepared for this brutal turn of events.

Upon hearing the news, Rigoberta's village decided that it was time to implement their plans. The villagers knew that they could not match the army's machine guns and heavy weapons, but they could defend themselves against units that came on foot to kidnap and raid the village. A community meeting was called. Villagers came armed with ideas. For generations, the Mayans had resisted Spanish conquerors, and the villagers would use those same techniques to defend themselves again.

The first meeting was very emotional because everyone realized that they could be kidnapped, tortured, or murdered at any time. After praying to God for help and for permission to use parts of the natural world to defend themselves, the residents of Chimel made their plans. Every idea was carefully evaluated for success: Would the plan work? What would the children do? Who would teach them their parts? What would the men do? What would the women do? Planning was complicated, because every possible alternative had to be considered. Their lives depended on it.

In the end, the villagers decided to communicate by secret signals. They would spend the next two months building a large house so they could live closer together.

Construction would include emergency exits to safe hiding places in the mountains, where provisions would be stored for long periods in hiding.

No roads led to their village, everyone came and went on foot through the jungle. Villagers planned to surprise would-be attackers by constructing a series of hidden traps. They dug deep ditches and covered them with leaves. Every villager knew exactly where each trap was located. Lookouts were posted 24-hours a day. Children manned the lookouts in the daytime, and two adults were posted at each one after dark.

Because soldiers who came to kidnap and murder did not dress in uniform, villagers were told what to watch for. If the army came, lookouts would signal villagers one way in the daytime and another at night. The men would exit the village and head immediately to the mountain hideouts. Although the women might be beaten or raped, it was the men who generally were kidnapped by the soldiers and never seen again.

Village women knew how to protect themselves. Lime juice squirted into the eyes of an attacker could blind. They also armed themselves with sprays made from hot chilies, water, salt, and lime.

Every object was considered as a possible weapon. Even the Bible proved useful. Especially inspiring were the stories of those who triumphed over more powerful foes. The Bible stories were full of helpful suggestions, especially the story of Moses, who freed his people from oppression, and the David and Goliath story, in which a shepherd boy defeated the king

Villagers made their own catapults, slingshot-type de-vices from which they could shoot stones at approaching soldiers. They made explosives by sticking a lighted wick into a lemonade bottle filled with petrol, oil, and iron filings. Every villager was armed with stones, machetes, and sticks.

Many of the soldiers who kidnapped and killed villagers were Indians from other parts of Guatemala. They had been captured by the military and forced to search out and kill guerrillas in the mountains. These soldiers feared the guerrilla forces who were said to be fierce fighters. None of the soldiers expected what they found in Chimel.

When the army finally came to Rigoberta's village, the people were ready. Lookouts signaled the soldiers' coming, and village men fled to the hideouts. Finding no men to kidnap, the soldiers prepared to depart but not before killing village dogs to show their frustration. As the soldiers began to depart, villagers sprang into action. They took their cue from the Bible story of Judith, a woman who used her beauty to lure her enemy into a trap.

A pretty young Mayan girl flirted with one of the last straggling soldiers. Taken by her beauty, he stopped to ask her where all the villagers went. When he looked up, the other soldiers were gone and he was surrounded. Rigoberta was one of the first to jump out at him. Another villager bumped him from behind, knocking him off balance. A third shouted," Don't move; hands up! Drop your weapons!" Thinking he was surrounded, he surrendered.

Now the villagers had weapons: a rifle, a pistol, and grenades—none of which they knew how to use. The soldier was blindfolded and taken to the village house. There he was dressed in Indian clothes and tied up. They wanted him to look like everyone else in case the soldiers returned for him.

Village mothers scolded him for becoming a soldier and killing Indians like himself. They told him how difficult it was for a mother to bring a son into the world. It made them sad to see this Indian boy become their enemy. They begged him to make the other soldiers stop the violence and they told him to deliver their message to the Guatemalan army: "We will fight till the last drop of blood to resist your campaign against us."

Rather than kill the soldier, the villagers decided to release him even though the army might retaliate against them. After a few hours, he returned to his unit. The villagers were thrilled at their victory. They were relieved and encouraged that they could so easily capture a soldier and take his weapons.

A few days later, word came that the soldier had been killed. When he didn't return with the others, they assumed he had been captured by the guerrillas. But when he turned up in Indian clothes and without his weapons, they suspected he was an informer and killed him.

Word spread that the village of Chimel was ready to fight back, and the army did not return. Neighboring villages were not so lucky. Rigoberta heard the story of four young Indian girls from a nearby village who had been brutally raped. Two were pregnant and in great despair over the unwanted babies they carried. The other two were recovering slowly from a brutal attack by five soldiers. Rigoberta knew she had to do something to protect her people.

Soon she began to teach self-defense in the village of Cortal. There she encountered a woman who had recently moved to the village. The woman was 90 years old, which was very unusual because Guatemalan Indians generally die young as a result of poor living conditions and malnutrition.

The old woman told a remarkable story. Her husband had left home one day and never returned. He had been killed by soldiers or finca police. Then her son disappeared, and another son went to find him. Neither of them returned. A third son went to find out what had happened to his father and brothers. He too disappeared. One by one, all of her sons vanished. She was all alone when she came to Cortal and asked to become part of the village.

The villagers of Cortal wanted to defend their town and to provide special protection for this old woman. They dug deep traps at the doors of each house, but instead of staying in their homes, they decided to post lookouts and sleep in the mountains. The old woman, however, could not take the mountain cold and dampness. She insisted on remaining in her home. "If they kill me, they kill me," she said. "I have no family, no husband, no children, no grandchildren."

The traps were left open in the daytime and set and covered at night. Every evening, the villagers returned to the mountains. The old lady set her traps; gathered her machete, axe, hoe, and stones; and drifted off to asleep.

In the middle of the night, villagers were awakened by the lookouts. The soldiers were coming. The lookouts waved lighted torches to tell how many soldiers were approaching. Everyone was afraid for the old lady. Soon the village dogs began to bark and shots rang out. Not a sound came from the old woman.

It was quiet for a long time. Then the lookout signaled again. The soldiers were leaving the village. They were sure the old lady was dead, but according to the lookout, fewer soldiers left the village than had arrived. The villagers watched and waited for the rest of the night.

Early the next morning, the old woman hobbled excitedly toward the hideout. She was laughing and crying at the same time. At first everyone was happy to see her. Then they became suspicious: How could she have survived unless she were an "ear" who sold out to the government for money? The villagers knew that if the woman were an informer, they would have to kill her. To do otherwise would endanger them all.

At the entrance to the hideout, the old woman shouted, "I've killed a soldier." She held up a rifle and pistol. She explained that when the soldiers entered the village, she slipped out of her house armed with an axe. One soldier sidestepped the trap at her door. She crept up behind him as he peeked inside. She hit him in the head with the axe. The other soldiers found his body and panicked. Thinking it was the work of guerrilla fighters, they fled in fear.

In his haste to escape, another soldier fell into her trap. The villagers could hardly believe their ears. One tiny 90-year-old woman had defeated the army. She lifted the rifle and said, "This is what killed my children. Now we can defend ourselves."

Upon returning to Cortal, villagers found that the soldier who had been struck by the axe was dead. Apparently, he had also been shot by another soldier. The villagers gathered around the soldier in the trap. They told him to give up his weapons and they would pull him from the hole. He too was an Indian from a distant village. "How can you kill your own people?" they asked him.

Village girls taunted the soldier. They accused him of being a monster like the soldiers who had raped and beaten them. The soldier broke down and cried. He told the villagers that he was just following orders. He too had been kidnapped from his home town and forced into the military. His superiors told him how stupid his parents were. They taught him to speak Spanish. They hit him and ordered him to kill the enemies of Guatemala.

The "enemies" were the guerrilla fighters who hid in the mountains and anyone else who wanted land reform or political changes in Guatemalan society. The young soldier feared that the army might one day tell him to kill his own family. But if he tried to quit, they would kill him first.

The villagers persuaded him to put down his arms and go into hiding. This gave them hope. If they could convince one soldier to abandon the army, perhaps they really could bring about dramatic changes. In their excitement, they were able to forget for a moment that there were many more soldiers waiting in the darkness.

CHAPTER 9: PETROCINO

*"When a woman sees her son tortured, burned
alive, she is incapable of forgiving, incapable
of getting rid of her hate."*

Rigoberta went to work for the Committee of United
Campesinos (CUC) in 1979. Her job was to travel throughout the region and organize Indians in remote villages and
on fincas. The peasant's union had existed publicly only
since 1978 and had never been officially recognized by
the government. Its goals were fair wages for all workers; decent treatment for Indians; and respect for Indian
culture, customs, and religion.

The CUC condemned the killing of 106 men, women,
and children in the village of Panzos in May 1978. Peasants had been murdered for refusing to leave their lands—
lands on which rich oil deposits recently had been discovered. On occasion, the union called for strikes and
demonstrations against landowners who would not pay
workers the legal minimum wage. The union also crit-
icized the government's ban on religious ceremonies in
Indian villages it considered to be pro-guerrilla.

The government responded to union efforts by declar-
ing the CUCs activities illegal. This meant that everyone involved in the CUC now was an enemy of the state.
Rigoberta's family could be arrested at any moment. For
their own safety and for the safety of their hosts, they
stayed with different families every night and were constantly on the move.

Even Rigoberta's youngest brother, Petrocino, was far
from a typical carefree 16-year-old boy. As secretary of
the village, he was a responsible member of the adult

community. In addition to teaching villagers self-defense and safety measures, he enjoyed being a catechist like his sister Rigoberta.

On September 9, 1979, all that changed. Sunday afternoon as he traveled with two other villagers, Petrocino was kidnapped by the army. As his companions watched in horror, soldiers tied Petrocino's hands behind his back and pushed him over rough stony ground, kicking him over and over again as he fell. By the time he reached the military camp near the village of Chajul, his face so badly swollen and bleeding that he was nearly unrecognizable.

When Juana heard the news, she rushed to the authorities to inquire about her son. This was very dangerous because she too could have been arrested at any time. Juana learned that Petrocino had been betrayed by an "ear," a man who worked in the village but could not resist the lure of 15 quetzals or two weeks' pay—the government's bounty for information leading to the arrest of a village leader. The soldiers did not even know who Petrocino Menchú was until he was brought to army headquarters and identified.

Petrocino was interrogated for hours and tortured mercilessly. "Where is your family? Are village priests and nuns working with the guerrillas? Why do you carry a Bible? Who in your community is helping the guerrillas?"

Each time Petrocino refused to answer, a fingernail was torn from his bleeding hands. Still Petrocino refused to implicate others—even as his captors used their crude weapons to peel strips of hair and skin from his skull. For three days, Petrocino's agony continued, but his torturers were careful not to kill him.

On September 23, soldiers posted notices throughout

the area that captured guerrillas would be punished at 11 o'clock the next morning at the military camp near Chajul. Villagers were instructed to come and witness the punishment or they too would be arrested. The Menchús knew that the soldiers hoped to scare villagers and keep them from joining the CUC and supporting the guerrilla movement. They knew it was a no-win situation: Not attending the public meeting could result in their own deaths, but attending might get them killed just as quickly. They left immediately for the overnight trip through the mountains to be with Petrocino.

When they arrived, Chajul was an armed camp with jeeps, armored cars, and 500 soldiers equipped with every kind of weapon. Helicopters flew overhead as twenty men and one woman were paraded before the crowd. Some had no ears, others had no tongues. The Menchús hardly recognized Petrocino. His head was swollen, and he had been beaten severely.

To Rigoberta, he seemed barely alive. But Juana would never forget the look of total recognition on his face and a wry little smile for her. Each victim had suffered horribly and could barely stand. The crowd of neighbors, friends, and family wept. For two hours, the officer in charge lectured the Indians on the evils of the guerrilla movement. He chastised villagers for not being satisfied with their lives and promised to torture anyone who participated in guerrilla activities.

As Rigoberta looked at the people around her, she was most frightened by the rage and resolve on her father's face. He did not shed a single tear, but his face told of his excruciating pain at seeing his child suffer so much. Petrocino had done nothing to deserve such torture, and

Vincent could do nothing to stop it.

As family members restrained Juana from running to Petrocino's side, the unthinkable happened. Soldiers lined up the prisoners one by one, poured gasoline on them, and set them afire. The horrified crowd rushed toward their loved ones only to pull back as the soldiers drew their weapons and shouted in unison: " Viva Guatemala," as if they had somehow scored a savage victory.

Some in the crowd scrambled for buckets of water. But it was too late. Half dead from grief, Juana was finally able to hold and kiss her son one last time. Rocking him gently, she told him through her tears how much she loved him. As families began to claim the bodies, the crowd began to disperse, and the Menchús started their long agonizing journey home. Rigoberta was numb, but her mind kept racing: If the Bible says it's a sin to kill, how can the government do this?

For the next few weeks, Petrocino was constantly on Juana's mind. She remembered how sick he had been as a baby, and how she had struggled to buy medicine for him only to watch him die in agony at age 16. She gathered his clothes to give to friends in the mountains and she vowed never to forgive Petrocino's murderers.

Despite all their pain and suffering, the Menchús never considered giving up their struggle for human rights. Petrocino's death was a horror that made each family member more committed and more determined to fight on. Though they never discussed it, each one found and followed their own path to involvement.

Rigoberta's younger sister joined the guerrillas. Vincent returned to his organizing work and urged his children to renew their commitments to the cause in memory of those who had given their blood. Juana cried for the thousands of mothers who, like her, would suffer the loss of their children. She dedicated herself to working with mothers and teaching them about the peasant movement.

Rigoberta was so confused that she left home. She had been working with a ladino in the CUC, an educated man who was helping her improve her Spanish. His friendship and respect had taught her that not all ladinos were evil. She began to see that discrimination was the tool that allowed the wealthy landowners to keep ladinos and Indians apart and thus control them both. To change this system, Rigoberta would have to think differently about ladinos and work toward a day when ladinos and Indians could work together for change. It was the system she hated, not ladinos.

Rigoberta returned to work with the CUC. Her job was to go out and talk to peasants and then share their ideas and opinions with the central organization. She worked long hours and was constantly afraid and lonely. She was rarely able to see the most important people in her life— her family. Little did she know that within a year of Petrocino's murder, she would find herself even more alone.

CHAPTER 10: VINCENT

"We must all give our lives, I know—but not altogether. Let it be one at a time so that someone is left, even if it's only one of our family."

Rigoberta saw her father for the last time in November 1979. They spent two days catching up on what the other had been doing. Vincent encouraged Rigoberta in her work, and Rigoberta marveled at how successfully her father had combined being a good Christian and leading his people in the fight against injustice. Vincent told Rigoberta that he hoped there would be no more deaths or martyrs for the cause.

After Petrocino's death, however, the violence in and around El Quiché grew worse. During his visit, Vincent told Rigoberta that seven village leaders from San Miguel Uspantan had been kidnapped. About 100 peasants were planning to gather in the capital to protest the kidnappings.

Four large landowners controlled employment around the village of San Miguel Uspantan. The seven who were kidnapped had staged a work-stoppage at one of the fincas because the owner refused to pay the legal minimum wage. The landowners encouraged the kidnappings in hopes of discouraging the peasants' fight for better wages.

Tension between landowners and workers had grown worse because soldiers who were stationed in the area became increasingly frustrated at not finding any guerrillas and began randomly killing Indians. The soldiers didn't seem to care how many innocent Indians died. They only hoped that some of the dead—or even one—were guerrilla sympathizers.

When more than 100 peasants gathered in Guatemala City to protest the kidnappings, the government did not even respond. Eventually most of the protestors had to return home to their villages. Vincent and the CUC decided on a second demonstration. They demanded that the government investigate the kidnappings in San Miguel Uspantan. They also protested the presence of so many soldiers in the area and their brutal actions.

Many citizens of Guatemala City, especially the students from San Carlos University, supported the Indians' right to demand a response from the government. Early in this second demonstration, protesters received word that the seven village leaders had been found dead. The crowd quickly got out of hand, and one supporter was killed.

Protest leaders knew that a peaceful demonstration attracting international attention was their only hope. On January 31, 1980, 22 peasants, including Vincent Menchú, occupied the Spanish Embassy. They carried no firearms. Their goal was to be exiled as political refugees and tell the world about the Indians' plight in Guatemala.

The embassy seemed a safe place from which to confront the government. The peasants anticipated support there because the Spanish ambassador had listened sympathetically over the years whenever Spanish priests' related incidents of military violence.

The Spanish ambassador asked the police not to interfere that day, but as he and a former vice-president and foreign minister of Guatemala met with the Indians, the embassy was bombed. The building was consumed by fire. Only the ambassador and one peasant, Gregorio Yuja Zona, survived the attack. Zona was later kidnapped from the hospital and killed, his body dumped on the San Carlos University campus as a warning to anyone who supported the peasants' rights organization. Spain immediately broke off diplomatic relations with Guatemala.

Rigoberta wanted to die. She knew that her father was dead and she had heard rumors that her mother and brothers were also at the embassy. She could not bear the thought of losing her father, let alone her entire family. The victims' bodies were so badly burned that identification was slow and difficult. Not until later did Rigoberta learn that her family had tried to join Vincent at the embassy, but the CUC refused to allow them to come in case the situation was more dangerous than they expected.

Rigoberta knew that her father had been prepared to die for what he believed in, but she was devastated at the thought of not seeing him again. Rigoberta's special bond with her father was forged when she was just a little girl, lost and alone in the mountains for more than seven hours. While collecting wood, she had become separated from her father, brothers and sister. Vincent was frantic at the disappearance of his youngest child. As he and the family searched the jungle for her, black storm clouds gathered overhead. The jungle could not have been a more ominous and threatening place. But what Rigoberta remembered most about that day was not the darkness or her fear, but the look on Vincent's face when they were reunited. She realized then for the first time how important she was to him. From that day forward, Rigoberta carried something vital within her.

Many years later, Vincent told Rigoberta how proud he was of her courage, how smart she was, and how he had regretted not allowing her to go to school. Vincent always helped Rigoberta with her problems and often found a way to make her believe in herself. She would miss him terribly.

Vincent Menchú had become a martyr for the cause and a national hero. His death and the deaths of the others at the embassy outraged many Guatemalans who responded at their funerals with an outpouring of sympathy. Vincent's death did what so many others had been unable to do: It attracted world attention to the Guatemalan Indians' struggle for human rights.

In addition to Vincent, the village of Chimel had lost eight others in the embassy fire, all close friends of the Menchús. Those who remained were so fearful that they lived in hunger rather than venturing out to the market for food. Rigoberta was thrown into a panic upon hearing that her mother had returned to help her neighbors in Chimel. Within a few months, Rigoberta would again come face to face with death.

CHAPTER 11: JUANA

"My people need me and here is where I have to be."

After Petrocino's death, Juana tucked her sorrow deep into her heart and plunged herself into her work. She traveled from village to village to "politicize mothers." Juana was a monument to the suffering they all endured. Rather than lecturing young mothers at village community centers, Juana worked alongside them as they prepared tortillas, made dinner, and cared for their children. She helped with their work on the milpas, and she taught them by example how to organize for their own protection. She told them that victory for all Indians required their involvement.

The struggle was beginning to take a new turn. In February 1980, sugar and cotton plantation workers in the Boca Costa region organized a strike that crippled the national economy for 15 days. A work stoppage that began with 8,000 peasants eventually grew to nearly 80,000. Workers were demanding a minimum wage of five quetzals a day ($5) and better living conditions. Machines were sabotaged, and many workers were killed.

The Indians were learning that change demanded personal risk-taking. Real change would not come from paper shufflers speaking on their behalf.

The landowners eventually settled for a minimum wage of three quetzals and twenty centavos a day, but many did not keep their word. The government was becoming alarmed by the Indians' coordinated efforts. The army began to fire bomb houses and use napalm grenades to burn crops and children who stumbled across the grenades as they played. The Guatemalan army was involved in a full-blown war with its own people.

Juana was once more the healer, attending to the many who lost hands and eyes in the bombings or who were badly burned. She took care of children whose parents disappeared or were killed. Instead of organizing peasants, she spent her days training others to do her job in case something should happen to her.

When word reached Juana that her fellow villagers could not even risk venturing out to the market, she returned home. Outsiders offered to help get her out of the country, but she refused to go. Rigoberta loved hearing villagers tell of her mother's courage. She was proud of how brave Juana was, and each story reassured her that her mother was well and safe. Hearing that Juana had returned home, however, greatly alarmed Rigoberta.

On April 19, 1980, as Juana returned from shopping for the village at a nearby market town, she was kidnapped. Juana was taken to a camp, beaten, and raped. Her head was shaved and she was dressed in a military uniform and taunted by soldiers, "If you are so sympathetic to the guerrillas, fight us now."

After days of torture, her ears were cut off. When she was close to death, her clothing was sent to the town hall in Uspantan as evidence of her capture. When friends inquired about her, the soldiers told them that she wanted to see her children before she died.

Rigoberta and her brothers and sisters wept at the news. Although they knew that going to see their mother would result in their own deaths, they longed to be with her. The family's grief was further intensified by the helplessness of knowing that for every moment that passed, their mother continued to be tortured.

When Juana finally died, Rigoberta was sad and yet relieved. But even in death there was no peace. The soldiers made sure that Juana's family could not give her a proper Mayan burial. Her captors guarded her remains for four months until Juana's body had decomposed and little trace of her was left.

CHAPTER 12: THE ORPHANS' STORY

"When you're in danger and you know you've only a minute of your life left, you don't remember what you did yesterday, or what you're going to do tomorrow."

After Juana died, Rigoberta was in a state of severe depression. She had worked with the CUC, which now had united with other groups to form the 31st of January Popular Front. The name change commemorated the date on which Vincent and the others had died at the Spanish Embassy.

On a daily basis, peasants set up boycotts and strikes and tampered with equipment to slow down production on the fincas of landowners who continued unfair labor practices. Rigoberta was a member of the "lightening meetings." These were quick, unannounced public forums held on street corners in the capital. A group of activists from the Popular Front would set up barricades and block traffic. They handed out leaflets describing their grievances with the landowners or the government's human rights abuses and then announced a time and place for future protests.

While the activists were talking to the gathering crowd, another member of the group would call police. By the time the police arrived, the group would have dispersed and the activists would have gone on to another location. This form of protest was designed to frustrate the police and leave them always one step behind the protesters.

By becoming a public figure, Rigoberta had also become a hunted woman. The army now knew what she looked like and was actively searching for her and her brothers. She lived on the run and slept in a different location each night. Her greatest fear was that a government spy would turn her over to police.

The constant tension made her sick. She developed an ulcer, and sometimes she felt as if she couldn't go on. Rigoberta thought a lot about what it was like to be an orphan. She identified with the thousands of Guatemalan children who had been orphaned during the struggle for human rights and were unable to tell their own stories. No matter how hard she tried to put the bloodshed out of her mind, she could never forget such painful memories.

One day at a chance meeting, she ran into her little sister, whom she hadn't seen in four years. Her sister was 12 years old and had joined the guerrillas. Rigoberta was thrilled to see her and amazed at her composure and maturity. She listened to Rigoberta's despair and shared her thoughts about their family and their sorrows.

The two sisters talked about what good people their parents had been and how they had cherished their family and friends. Even though their parents had never killed anyone or taken anything that didn't belong to them, they were brutally murdered.

"We have to fight without measuring our suffering...or thinking about the monstrous things we must bear in life," her sister said. Our parents have given us the greatest reason to continue. A revolutionary is not born of peace and privilege, but of injustice and bitterness, her sister reminded her. She encouraged Rigoberta to go on fighting.

Rigoberta was revitalized by the meeting. That night, she dreamed about her parents. They came to her and told her that she was capable of many things. Then Vincent turned to her and said, "You are a woman. That's enough of that." As always, Vincent was able to raise her spirits.

Rigoberta had been staying with supportive and encouraging friends, but she was a great danger to them. Talking stopped whenever a truck or jeep passed by their house. Breathing stopped when the truck or jeep came to a halt.

One day as Rigoberta walked down the street with a girlfriend, a military jeep passed her and a soldier called her name. When Rigoberta glanced up, the jeep then screeched to a halt and quickly made a U-turn. In a split second, Rigoberta's life flashed before her. She knew that she had many things left to do. She ducked into a passageway and darted into a church.

Without a word, Rigoberta quickly surveyed the scene. She removed her traditional headdress and released her long dark hair over her shoulders and down her back. Squeezing her eye closed, she knelt to pray alongside a stranger; her friend crossed the alter and knelt next to another woman. The soldiers entered the church, guns drawn. In their haste to find two Indian women on the run, they ignored the small groups kneeling in the church. They assumed that the "fugitives" had run out the side door and into the nearby market.

Rigoberta was frozen with fear. Then she remembered the many times she had wanted to die rather than go on. She knew now that it was better to live. She survived that day with a stronger-than-ever commitment to the struggle of her people.

Within days, Rigoberta escaped to Guatemala City. There she worked in a convent where no one knew her true identity. Slowly she recovered from her close call.

Her friends continued to insist that she leave the country for just a little while, and in the end, she agreed. She left for Mexico to regain her energy, feeling defeated, but knowing that she would be back.

The airplane ride to Mexico City was one of many "firsts" for Rigoberta. She met people from all over the world. Wherever she went, she carried the stories of the many Guatemalan orphans. A Canadian woman, who was involved with the Guatemalan Indians and knew about Rigoberta's story, set up a meeting between Rigoberta and her friend, anthropologist and writer Elisabeth Burgos-Debray, who was originally from Venezuela.

In January 1982, Rigoberta went to Paris as a representative of the 31st of January Popular Front. There she met Burgos-Debray. Together these two Latin American women spent a week taping Rigoberta's life story. In 1983, *I, Rigoberta Menchú, An Indian Woman In Guatemala* was published in Spanish, Rigoberta's second language. Finally, in Rigoberta's own words, the world learned all that had happened to her family and her culture. Finally, the world would know the story of all Guatemalan orphans.

CHAPTER 13: A NEW KIND OF LEADER

"We who were born when the war was born have never experienced a Christmas without war."

For the next 10 years, Rigoberta returned to Guatemala only a few times and always in hiding. She was sad at not being able to visit family and friends, but she knew that life in Guatemala was still too dangerous. Death threats were common.

Rigoberta continued to work with the peasants union and struggled with her own personal issues. She began to wonder whether she would ever have a "normal" family life again. She believed as all Mayans do that the earth gives food and woman gives life and that both are essential to the circle of life.

She knew she was old enough to be married. She had been in love several times, but the time for marriage never seemed quite right. She knew from experience how difficult raising a family could be, especially given the dangerous circumstances of her life.

Despite these painful realities, she sometimes daydreamed about having children. She knew that in the Guatemalan highlands, women often were widowed and left alone to raise many children in poverty. Although she longed to have children of her own, Rigoberta worried what would happen to them if she were to die? On the other hand, what joy would there be in any accomplishment, if she had no one with which to share her triumphs? She had many questions about her future but no answers.

Rigoberta concluded that for a while longer her commitments to her people had to take priority over personal happiness. Sometimes she struggled with even the most mundane things. For example, some of the men she worked with felt that their ideas were superior to any woman's. Some of them had problems taking direction from a woman. Others did not want their wives to participate in union activities.

Rigoberta spent a lot of time talking to men and women about these issues. At one point she decided that the best way to settle gender differences was to form a separate organization for women. But after considering this notion, she decided that as long as women picked cotton, coffee, and sugar cane alongside men—and as long as they were exploited just like men—women had a rightful place fighting for justice alongside men.

During her exile in Mexico, Rigoberta lived in poverty with other Mayan refugees. Many displaced Guatemalans lived in Mexico. They had all fled to safety and were awaiting return to their homeland. During these years, Rigoberta met people from all over the world. Many had read her book and knew of her family's struggle. Her story interested college students in particular. They were amazed that this simple peasant woman with no money or education had accomplished so much.

Rigoberta was earning a reputation as a diplomat and a peacemaker. She helped found the United Representation of the Guatemalan Opposition, an organization that petitioned the United Nations to support peace talks between the Indians and the Guatemalan government and condemned human rights abuses in her country.

Rigoberta was the narrator of *When the Mountains Tremble,* a film depicting the struggles of the Mayan people. Then, in 1986, she became a member of the National

Coordinating Committee of the CUC.

In October of 1992, the Nobel Committee announced that Rigoberta Menchú Túm would receive the Nobel Peace Prize on December 10 in Oslo, Norway. In addition to the prize, she would receive $1 million for use in furthering her work.

Rigoberta had been nominated for the award by Adolfo Perez Esquivel, the Argentine human rights advocate who won the prize in 1980. Rigoberta was in Guatemala at a gathering of indigenous people in the western town of San Marcos not too far from her own village when the announcement came. Upon hearing the news, her dark eyes shone brightly and a wide smile filled her round face. Her only wish was that her parents could have been there to share her joy.

Ironically, it was her own countrymen who protested her nomination the loudest. Enemies from the Guatemalan military and government came forward to defame her. Foreign Minister Gonzalo Menendez Park denounced her for openly criticizing her government. Others accused her of being a terrorist. From anonymous enemies, Rigoberta received bouquets of marigolds and baby's breath, traditional funeral flowers in Guatemala. After all that she had endured, even this well-deserved recognition came with a price: Death threats forced her to travel with a bodyguard.

On December 10, 1992, in a ceremony held in the exquisite Oslo Town Hall, before the King of Norway, the Norwegian Storting (parliament) and several hundred invited guests, Francis Sejersted, Chairman of the Norwegian Nobel Committee presented the Nobel Peace Prize to Rigoberta Menchú Túm in "recognition of her work for social justice and ethno-cultural reconciliation based on respect for the rights of indigenous peoples." Chairman Sejersted silenced her critics by saying that the committee was convinced that peace was the long-term objective of her struggle. She stands out as the shining symbol of that peace.

Rigoberta stood to receive this most prestigious prize barefoot and proudly dressed in the traditional Guatemalan ankle-length corte and multicolored huipil. She knew that Juana and Vincent would be proud of her. She was ready to continue her dreams.

With her cash award, Rigoberta founded the Vincent Menchú Foundation, established in honor of her father. With offices in Guatemala City, Mexico City, and New York City, one of the foundation's first undertakings was the purchase of land in Guatemala for the resettlement of Mayans who had fled to Mexico.

AFTERWORD

As a result of Rigoberta Menchú's ongoing work to ensure justice and equal rights for all indigenous people, the United Nations named her Ambassador of Indigenous Peoples for the Year 1993, the first year in the history of the U.N. to be declared International Year of Indigenous Populations.

The Vincent Menchú Foundation has been renamed the Rigoberta Menchú Tuḿ Foundation, because outside of Guatemala, Rigoberta is more well known than her father. Her status as a Nobel Prize winner has brought international attention to the foundation's work.

The foundation's primary focus has been to encourage Indians in Guatemala to become part of the political process by registering and voting and setting up educational programs for refugee children.

Rigoberta, once a shy Mayan girl, now mingles with people from around the world and encourages them— even celebrities—to become involved in the foundation's work. For example, Michael Stipe, lead singer for the rock group R.E.M., was so inspired by Rigoberta and her programs for young children that he designed a t-shirt to be sold at a foundation fundraiser.

Rigoberta has received honorary degrees from DePaul University in Chicago, the University of Saskatchewan in Saskatoon, Canada, and the National University of San Carlos in Guatemala. In Paris, she received the medal of the Legion of Honor from French President Jacques Chirac. She also was named the first world ambassador of Civicus, a new privately funded international organization whose mission is to help countries cultivate volunteerism and prod governments to do more for their citizens.

But even in the warm glow of the world spotlight, there are always struggles. Rigoberta cut short a speaking tour in the fall of 1995 and returned home to Guatemala to respond to a tragic situation. An army patrol had opened fire on citizens in the village of Xaman, a village founded by Mayan Indians who had resettled in their Guatemalan homeland with the help of the foundation.

Eight adults and three children had been killed. Rigoberta moved quickly to initiate legal action against the soldiers involved in the incident. Armed with legal counsel and a command of the language that Vincent never had, Rigoberta is now able to prod her government to answer her people's complaints.

Rigoberta still dreams of a better future, and some of her dreams have come true. She is married and lives in Guatemala City with her husband and young son, who has already begun to hear from his parents the stories of his ancestors.

The Nobel Prize

The Nobel Peace Prize is named for Alfred Nobel, a Swedish inventor who became one of the wealthiest men in Europe. Among his many inventions and patents is dynamite.

Alfred Nobel was a shy, lonely man who suffered from poor health. For most of his adult life, he was engrossed in scientific ideas, but he always dreamed of doing something more dramatic to "serve mankind."

Upon his death it was learned that he had made provisions in his will for his sizable fortune to be invested and to fund the Nobel Foundation. The interest on the foundation's investments would be awarded, "To persons whose work had been of the greatest benefit to mankind."

The first Nobel Peace Prize was awarded in 1901 and recognized Jean Henri Dunant, the Swiss founder of the Red Cross, and Frederic Passy of France, founder of the first French peace society. Each year thereafter, on December 10, the day Alfred Nobel died, the whole world awaits the committee's announcement of the five Nobel Prize recipients.

Specific Swedish agencies and institutes are commissioned to award prizes in chemistry, physics, medicine, and literature. The award for the champions of peace is made by a committee of five elected by the Norwegian Storting.

The Future

After 36 years of fighting, the civil war in Guatemala is coming to a end. Rigoberta Menchú and her generation of Guatemalans have never known a time without war. Since 1990, peace negotiations have stopped and started many times, ceasefires have been set and broken. But in December of 1996, the prospects for a real and lasting peace came to an impatient Guatemalan people tired of civil war.

Government and rebel representatives announced that by year's end a series of six separate agreements would be signed. They would address issues of human rights, Indian rights, poverty and land reform, constitutional reform, electoral procedures, and amnesty.

Rigoberta was jubilant at the first signing, which took place in the same town hall in Oslo where she received the Nobel Prize. However, for a generation of Guatemalan's who have known only war, hope is tempered by realism. Many new challenges remain as Guatemala moves toward democracy and justice. As one cautious Guatemalan man noted during the celebrations, "Peace is not born on paper; it is born in the heart."

Addendum

Even after winning the Nobel Prize, Rigoberta Menchú Túm's personal struggle continues. Shortly after receiving the prize, Rigoberta endured personal disappointment and embarrassment when several of her relatives staged a phony kidnapping for ransom. In 1996, Rigoberta was devastated when refugees in a relocation camp funded by her foundation were massacred. In 1998, Rigoberta and her husband suffered a most personal loss when their young son died unexpectedly.

Problems continued for Rigoberta in 1999, when a book by anthropologist David Stoll challenged details of her life as stated in her autobiography, *I, Rigoberta Menchú, An Indian Woman in Guatemala*. The very book, in fact, that provides much of the basis of this biography.

Although Geir Lundestad, director of the Norwegian Nobel Institute and permanent secretary of the Norwegian Nobel Committee, continues to express confidence in Rigoberta as a Nobel recipient, he also has explained that the Nobel Committee has made no effort to substantiate the charges or explain the inconsistencies because the autobiography was not the exclusive basis for awarding the prize to Rigoberta.

The author and publisher of this book reaffirm the position of the Nobel Committee, that details of Rigoberta's life may be in question, but no one has or can challenge her dedication and commitment to fighting for the rights of indigenous people—especially the Mayans of Guatemala.

RESOURCES

Find Out More

If you wish to receive the Rigoberta Menchú Tum Foundation newsletter or obtain information about Rigoberta's work and the work of her foundation, contact:

Rigoberta Menchú Tum Foundation-USA
    8 W. 40th St., Suite 1610
    New York, New York 10018-3902
    (212) 302-2139 & 302-2143
    Fax: 212/944-2678
    E-mail: rmtf@igc.apc.org
    Internet: http://ourworld.compuserve.com/
    homepages/rmtpaz

Sources

I, Rigoberta Menchú, An Indian Woman In Guatemala, Verso Publisher, USA and UK, 1984.

Champions of Peace by Tony Gray, Paddington Press Ltd., 1976.

Guatemala Central America's Living Past by Lila Perl, New York: William Morrow and Co., 1982.

The Gift of The Devil, A History of Guatemala by Jim Handy, Boston: South End Press, 1984.

Time Among the Maya by Ronald Wright, New York: Henry Holt and Co., 1991.

Other Items of Interest

Students who want to know more about peacemakers or the Mayans also may enjoy the following:

National Geographic—Lost Kingdom of the Maya, video-tape. (Available in public libraries and some video stores.)

Women of Peace, Nobel Prize Winners by Anne Schraff, Enslow Library, 1994.

Contemporary Profiles and Policy Series for the Younger Reader

This series provides a comprehensive biography of each person and a thorough discussion of the social and political issues reflected in their lives. International in scope, each book presents an account of the person's major accomplishments and an opportunity to review issues important to your life as a young person in today's world. Volumes currently published in the series are:

Sloane, Todd A. GONZALEZ OF TEXAS: A Congressman for the People. (ISBN 0-934272-37-9) (Cloth) (ISBN 0-934272-40-9) (Paper)

The background and life of this Congressman from Texas is as fascinating as any moving picture. Long a fixture in Texas politics, Henry B. Gonzalez was the first Mexican American elected to the United States Congress from the state. He has championed the underdog in politics throughout his career and has brought to national politics a keen analysis of major issues in foreign policy and economic affairs. The book features a personal interview with the Congressman for the young person.

Schulze, Julie. RIGOBERTA MENCHÚ TÚM: Champion of Human Rights. (ISBN 0-934272-42-5) (Cloth) (ISBN 0-934272-43-3) (Paper)

Winner of the Nobel Peace Prize (1992), this Quiché Indian woman from Guatemala is an heroine to the entire world. Using only the spoken and written word, Rigoberta Menchú Túm has brought social change to Guatemala and has been an inspiration to others far and wide. Raised in the most humble of surroundings, she had to learn Spanish as a second language to take up "words" as her weapons of choice in pursuit of social justice in Central America.

Myers, Nancy Cayton. NANCY LANDON KASSEBAUM: A Senate Profile. (ISBN 0-934272-47-6) (Cloth) (ISBN 0-934272-46-8) (Paper)

Born in a distinguished Kansas political family, this woman made history as the first woman in the United States Congress to head a major Senate Committee. In her role as chairperson of the Labor and Human Resources Committee, she co-sponsored and passed with Democratic Senator Edward M. Kennedy a bill which provides pioneering legislation for health insurance in the United States.

The series is published in paperback and in clothbound editions for library collections. Further information about these books and the series can be obtained from John Gordon Burke Publisher, Inc., PO Box 1492, Evanston, IL 60204-1492 U.S.A.